Trauma Informed Teaching Strategies that are Good for ALL!

Nathan Levy,
Dr. Melissa Sadin, &
Dr. James Singagliese

A Nathan Levy Books LLC Publication

A Note from the Author/Publisher – Nathan Levy

I have been providing activities for children to make them better thinkers and writers for more than fifty years (I was two years old when I started writing these activities – not really). In recent years, I have realized, thanks to my collaborations with my colleague Dr. Melissa Sadin, that many of these activities seem to be more impactful for those children with trauma symptoms. By putting our heads together and being joined by Dr. James Singagliese, we have compiled what we think is a series of activities that teachers can more safely use with children with trauma as well as all other children. I hope you have as much fun and satisfaction with the activities as we have had.

The Impact of Trauma on Learning

One in four children in every classroom, every day has experienced some type of trauma. Children who have prolonged exposure to trauma in childhood, including but not limited to family violence, physical, emotional or sexual abuse, separation from a primary care giver, and poverty are considered to have developmental trauma (DT). This type of trauma exposure may impair neurobiological development. The brains of children with prolonged trauma exposure may not be the same as children without trauma. Prolonged exposure to early childhood trauma causes atypical development of the amygdala, hippocampus, and prefrontal cortex. These important parts of our limbic system are necessary for, among other things, emotional control, language development, memory, and cognition.

In typical development, all children are amygdala driven at birth. The amygdala is also known as our survival brain. It is responsible for our survival behaviors. Human infants are completely unable to survive alone. If you put an infant in a field alone, s/he cannot survive. Babies cannot keep themselves warm. They cannot feed themselves. They cannot drink by themselves. They need another human to provide their basic needs. The amygdala is what causes babies to cry. They cry when they are hungry. They cry when they are thirsty. They cry when they are afraid. They cry when they are lonely. They cry as a way to bring another human to help them. If you have ever raised a baby or been close to someone who has, then you know that it is a pretty good system. When a baby cries, we respond. We pick him up. We ask him, "What's wrong?" We hold him, bounce him, check his diaper, check the time to decide if he is hungry or thirsty. While we are going through our checklist of what might be wrong, very often we are telling him that he will be all right. We tell him, "It's okay." When we do this over and over thousands of times over 2 to 3 years, the amygdala responds less, and the hippocampus gets busy. The hippocampus is the center for things such as self-regulation, language development, and memory. The activity in the hippocampus helps us realize that every discomfort is not life threatening. We can be hungry. It is okay. We will get food soon. We are cold. It is okay. We can get a coat or move to a warmer place. We begin to do for ourselves what our parents did for us when we were infants. Over the next 10 to 15 years, when we continue to have a safe place where our basic needs are met, our prefrontal cortex comes online. With the prefrontal cortex comes delayed gratification, choice, empathy, reasoning, and judgement.

Children with trauma have atypical limbic system development. Often, they do not get their basic needs met as infants and babies and toddlers. Their amygdala remains in charge. They are constantly on alert for perceived threats to their safety. With recent medical advances and the development of the functional magnetic resonance imaging (fMRI) machine, neurobiologists, scientists, and medical doctors have been able to study the response centers in the brains of living human subjects without endangering the safety of the subject. Research shows that children with trauma often have larger amygdala and smaller hippocampus volume than children without trauma. It is important to understand that this means that children in a 5th grade class may have the prefrontal cortex activity of a 4-year-old. High school students who have experienced trauma may have the judgement of a 5th grader. Brains cannot skip stages of development. A child cannot do more than their brain development allows. Children who are amygdala driven cannot choose their behavior. Sixteen-year-old young adults with DT may not choose a good peer group. They may not make age appropriate decisions while operating a vehicle.

They may not be able to wait their turn in class the way a child without trauma can.

Children with developmental trauma need to feel safe -- safe from judgement, punishment, and misunderstanding. With unconditional acceptance, they learn to establish relationships. Teachers can help children develop the ability to regulate their emotions through the creation of personal connections. When children with developmental trauma feel safe, they begin to connect with teachers. Children who are safe and connected are ready to learn. Children who are ready to learn are increasing prefrontal cortex activity.

Think About Maslow

In a paper about human motivation, Abraham Maslow introduced his hierarchy of needs. Maslow's hierarchy illustrates the stages that humans must move through to achieve self-actualization. Maslow explained that individuals could not skip stages and in order to move into the next level, individuals need to fully satisfy their current level.

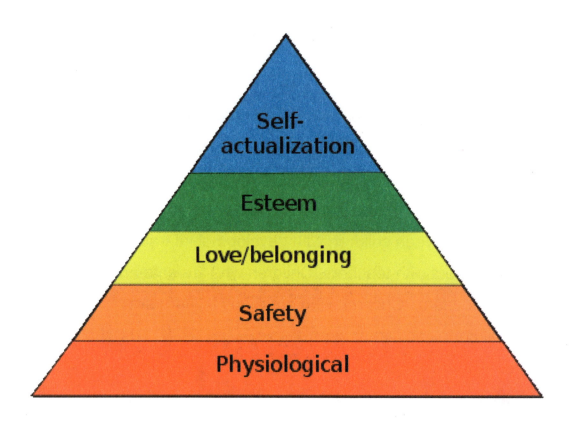

Similar to Maslow's hierarchy, individuals cannot skip stages of limbic system development. Children who do not get what they need remain driven by their amygdala. They cannot learn an activity that requires development in the hippocampus and prefrontal cortex, while they remain driven by their basic needs. Hungry children cannot learn effectively. Tired children are not efficient learners. Like Maslow's hierarchy predicts, children cannot learn unless we can provide their basic needs. After we assure that our students have food and rest, we need to help them feel safe and accepted in our classrooms. Then, and only then, can they learn. The strategies in this book have been shown to increase engagement and improve behavior and academic outcomes. These strategies will not be effective if you apply them to students who are hungry, tired, or unsafe.

#1

Greeting students by name and including a positive statement at the beginning of class increases engagement.

Relationship building language is one of the best ways to make connections with your students. A simple shift from "What's wrong with you?" to "What going on?" or "How can I help?" makes a huge difference in the way you are perceived by your students.

Greeting your students by name and making a positive statement that is NOT a judgement is key to establishing relationships that lead to students feeling safe.

For example – instead of "You look nice today." Try, "I'm glad you are here."

Student Behavior	Common Teacher Responses	What the Behavior Communicates	Relationship Building Response
Requiring undue attention – Calling out, talking over the teacher, engaging/distracting classmates, moving around the room in a distracting manner.	"Please sit down." Please stop doing that." "Pay attention." Irritation, frustration, anger may follow when the students does not comply, engage or respond.	"I don't belong." I feel invisible unless you are addressing me individually." "I am hyper aroused and cannot regulate myself." I need you to help me become and remain engaged in learning."	"I care about you and I need you to_____." Say what you mean and mean what you say. Say things once. Wait for compliance. "Show me what you should be doing." Ignore the behavior if it does not reach the level of unsafe. Give directions to the class. Then meet individually with the student. If you repeat this, the students will learn that she will get your attention. She will learn to wait.

Power Struggle – *"You are not the boss of me." "You can't make me."* **Insults your control or leadership of the classroom.**	*"I am in charge here." Asserting your dominance by making sure you win the argument. This may result in removing the students from your class or applying discipline in the form of detention or points.*	*"I feel so out of control." "I need to gain control." "I can't give you power because that is not safe for me." "I can't trust you to keep me safe."*	*Involve the student in the problem. Let them help. Acknowledge that you cannot make him or her do something. "I can't make you complete this assignment, but I need to know what you understand about the topic. How can we work together to solve this?" Give limited choices. "You can do this or that."*
Revenge – **"You will pay for this."** **"Threats against your safety of the safety of other students."**	Students who threaten violence or who act in unsafe ways often scare teachers. When we are scared, we respond by yelling, threatening discipline, holding (in the case of young children).	"I don't feel I belong." "I don't hear the same music everyone else hears." Misery loves company. I feel lonely or scared or worthless and I can only feel included when others feel lonely or scared or worthless	They are hurting. "Your behavior tells me you might be hurting. How can I help?" Ask questions. Stay calm and light. After the student is calm and safe, work with the child to develop a plan to fix what was broken – feelings, school property, the trust of classmates.
Worthlessness – **"I give up."** **"This is stupid. I can't do this."** **"I don't know."** **"I don't care."** **Head down, hoodie up.**	Teachers often start with encouraging statements. "You can do this." "Give it a try." However, when the student resists over a period of time, teachers become frustrated. They may threaten for lack of a better way to make the student comply. "If you don't do this assignment, you can't go out for recess."	"I am unworthy." "I have been thrown away." "I am helpless." "I have not developed the understanding that I can impact the direction of my day." Negative world view – "It's no good." "I give up."	Show them that they are worthy. Back up to what they do understand. Build slowly on that. Use active listening. "What I hear you saying is…" Give limited choices and show them the power of their decisions. "You chose to work on the algebra assignment. I see that you have many right answers. "Teach them to make a plan for a class period, Teach them to set & achieve short term goals.

One simple strategy used by Catia Kitchin, a kindergarten teacher in central New Jersey, is to greet her students at the door allowing them to choose the "welcoming." She posted various greetings at her door and, depending on the mood of the child, they may give her a high five, smile, hug, or hand shake. Not only does this provide an opportunity for the adult and child to connect, it also helps the teacher determine how each of his/her students are feeling that day. This quick simple strategy informs the teacher with valuable information about how to approach and engage individual students first thing in the morning.

There are many ways to greet your students that will allow them to feel welcomed and prepare their brains for the start of the school day. The website, "We are Teachers" (https://www.weareteachers.com/) provides free calendars with jokes, questions, and thought provoking statements that are great to help axon firing. An example is provided below---What are you thankful for?

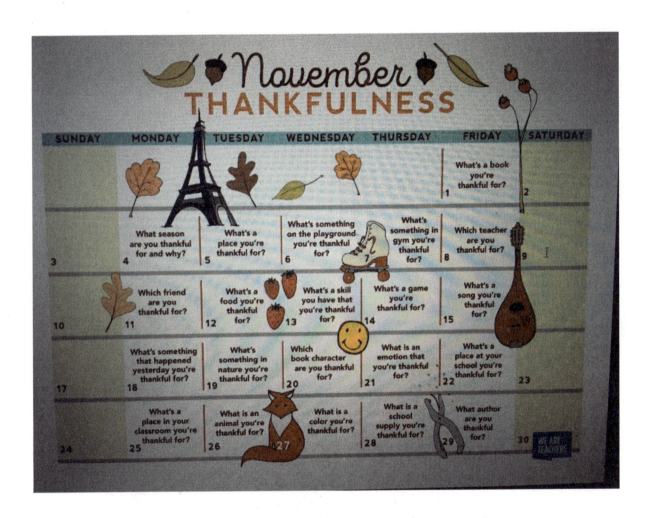

I Gotta Be Me...

People often say, "Be yourself." Explain if this is easy or hard for you to do. When are you most likely to be yourself? How do you feel when you are not acting like yourself?

The Me Nobody Knows...

"It is thus with most of us; we are what other people say we are. We know ourselves chiefly by hearsay." - Eric Hoffer

1. What do people say you are?
2. How does what they say compare to what you think you are?
3. There have been many experiments done to prove that what people think of themselves is strongly affected by the way they think others see them, and that, given the right circumstances, people will begin living up (or down) to other people's ideas of who they are. Consciously or unconsciously, individuals will change their personality to fit what other people are thinking about them. Why do you think this is true? Has this happened to you? If so, write about the experience. If not, write about how you've managed to avoid this situation.

Easy Off - Easy On...

What places, people, ideas and things are you interested in? Discuss why they appeal to you. What places, people, ideas and things are you not interested in? Discuss why they are unappealing. Based on this information, come up with one sentence that describes you.

Fame...

1. Would you like to be famous? Answer yes or no and explain your choice. Consider what it might be like to be famous - how it would affect your day-to-day existence and what you might have to sacrifice in order to obtain it.
2. Who do you think is the most famous person in the world? Explain.
3. "Fame is a magnifying glass." Explain how this is true.

First-Last...

What is the first thing you would like people to know about you? What is the last thing you would want people to know about you?

#2

Make learning relevant. Explain the importance of what the students are learning in their own lives.

EVEN BETTER – provide opportunities for them to tell you why what they are learning is important.

"If there is no meaning in it, that saves a world of trouble, you know, as we needn't try to find any."
King of Hearts in Alice in Wonderland, Lewis Carrol

Research suggests that effective learning enhances a student's understanding of classroom expectations and their value for learning. As such, educators are beginning to incorporate this philosophy into planning and executing classroom lessons. A strategy for this practice is requiring the classroom teacher and the student to effectively answer the following three questions during the learning process:

1. What am I learning?
2. Why is it important that I learn this?
3. How will I know I have learned it?

Provided below is an example from Ashley Hirt's classroom that utilizes the three student-focus questions as referenced above. Ashley is a general education teacher from New Jersey who collaborates with students to develop individualized learning goals.

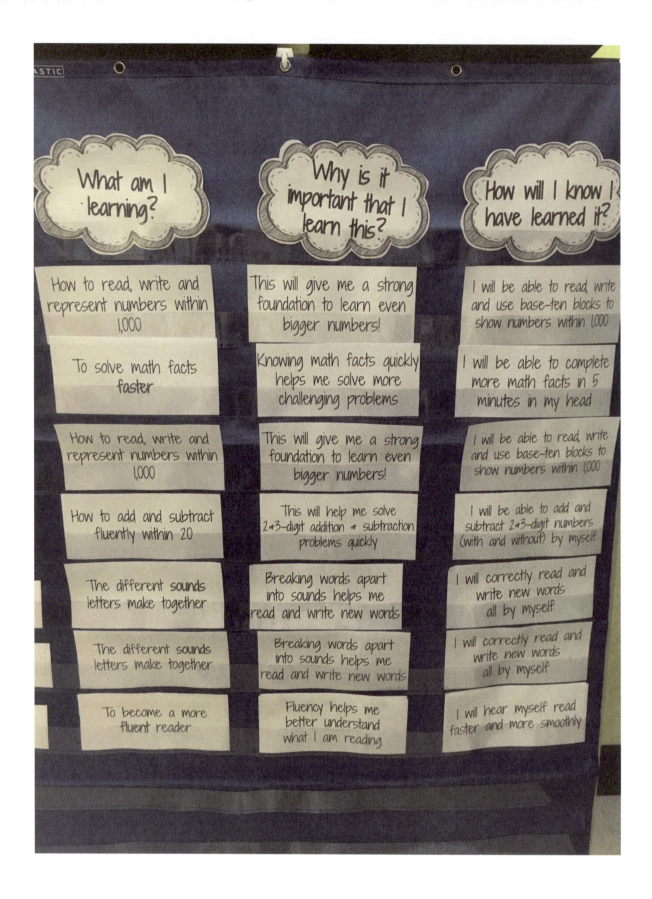

Sample Lesson Format...

Asking students why things are important to them creates a personal connection. Many children who have experienced early childhood trauma struggle to engage with material they do not see as important. The part of the brain that helps us maintain interest in things that do not relate to us is within the hippocampus and may not be developed as a result of the trauma.

Consider this middle school math lesson by Kristopher Scotto at Unity Charter School. In this lesson, Kris introduced the objective of the lesson. He used questions throughout the lesson and concluded the lesson by asking the students to tell him why they needed to learn "order of operations." This is true backward design. The students were engaged by the questions used throughout the lesson, and they enjoyed the discussion at the conclusion of the lesson.

Essential Question – Why do we complete tasks in a certain way?

Objective – Students will be able to solve order of operations problems with positive and negative integers. (Do not state this at the beginning of class. Use the essential question as your focus statement.)

Core Content Standards – 7.NS.2a, 7NS.2b, 7NS.2c

Do Now:

What are the two strategies you learned in order to divide fractions? What is 4/7 divided by 2/3? How can you check that your answer is correct?

Procedure:

Using the DO NOW as a guide, facilitate a discussion between the students about which of the two students from the DO NOW was correct or incorrect and why they thought that. They actually are both incorrect and the students should be comfortable explaining their reasoning and eventually explaining their solution to the problem (the next step). Students should be using language like "product, quotient, sum, difference, parentheses, negative, positive, evaluate, solution, justify." Give students a second example and show them how color-coding different operations can be helpful to show which operations are "high priority".

Closing Activity: Ask the students to identify the objective. What did we learn?

Easier Than What...

What would be easier for you to give up..

    Your cell phone or your gaming system?

What would be easier for you to do without…

    An allowance or all desserts?

What would be easier for you to say…

    I am sorry or I love you?

What I Know...

Write at least one paragraph about something you know about that your teacher does not know about.

This activity can be done as an exploratory activity to introduce a new topic. "List or write a paragraph showing all that you know about _____." This will help create a personal connection for your students and also give you an idea of what your students know and do not know about a topic.

Nicely Done...

Write one paragraph for each:

> The nicest thing I ever did for anyone…
>
> The nicest thing anyone ever did for me…
>
> The nicest thing I ever did for myself…

Substitute Teacher...

List four famous people (dead or alive) that you would like as a substitute teacher. Explain your choices.

Why Worry...

What are things you think (or know) grownups worry about?

What things do children your age worry about?

What is the same or difference about their worries? Do the worries fit any categories or patterns?

What is something you think everyone worries about? What makes it a universal worry?

Hearing Aid...

Choose two of the following to write about or discuss:

Words people need to use more often.

Words people need to use less often.

Things I was glad I said.

Things I heard but did not understand.

Things I thought I heard but really did not

#3

Proximity is important. Some students need to be close to you. When students who struggle with learning are asked to move to the front row, their participation and academic performance is improved.

Strategies for maintaining proximity...

- If the student responds well to it, put an occasional hand on their shoulder as you pass by.

- For the younger students, allow students who need to sit at your feet, or as is appropriate, on your lap. For older students, position yourself near the students. Walk among them.

- Put your desk against the wall. Avoid sitting behind it. Teach from round or kidney shaped tables.

- If you have carpet and you are physically able, sit on the carpet with students. Sit at desks and at tables with middle and high school students.

- Allow for flexible seating. Tall desks, low desks, standing tables, soft seating.

- When you are working from a white board or SMART board, put students who respond to proximity near the board.

- Walk around and stand in different parts of the room as you speak and teach.

On the Average...

What is your definition of average?

Tell about something that is above average?

Tell about something that is below average?

What is positive/negative about being average?

Evaluate: What is average about you? (Consider: appearance, height,
weight, athletic ability, intelligence, etc.)

Or Is It?

"Life isn't fair!"

Make an argument in favor of this statement...

and then...

Make an argument against this statement.

How...

How can someone move away from you while standing still?

How can a victory be a loss?

How can a mask be revealing?

Power Play...

What is more powerful...ideas or actions?

Give two examples to prove your point.

Puzzles...

Which is worse...a pimple or an insult?

Which is colder...ice or being left out?

Use specific examples to support answer.

#4

Test to teach. Take practice tests. This reduces stress related knowledge loss. Ask students to use what you want them to know. Give open book/computer tests.

Testing, 1, 2, 3...

What do you think of tests? Would you like to abolish them? State the good things/bad things about tests.

If you did not have exams, do you think you would work harder or not? How would your study habits change?

What advice would you give a friend before an important test?

What kind of tests do people have to face in life, outside of school?

What are some alternatives to traditional exams? Give some ideas.

Maybe ...

Have the students develop a study guide. This provides an excellent review of the test content. In addition, having students generate questions about content develops connections in the hippocampus which will improve emotional regulation in all students!!! Avoid over practicing for a test. When students were given twenty practice math problems, they scored better than when they were given fifty practice problems. Results showed that students began to make mistakes after about problem # 25, thus dragging down their overall score. Children with trauma often demonstrate cognitive fatigue. LESS IS MORE!

Write ten questions that you would answer

Yes to

Write ten questions that you would answer

No to

Then, answer this question:

Are you more **yes, no or maybe**? **Why**?

When is quantity important?

When is quality important?

Which do you have more of in your life...quantity or quality?

Would you rather have quantity or quality when it comes to: friends,

family, food, video games, time with family???

To Teach Or...

If you teach and nobody learns, have you taught? Explain.

Don't Ask Me...

Answer each in a paragraph.

Do I have to know it for the test?

Does spelling count?

How long should it be?

Do I have to finish it for homework?

#5

For cognitively demanding tasks, students should avoid background noise (i.e., from computers, TV and music players) and should avoid social media.

Strategies for reducing background noise…

- Play soft music in your classroom when students are working independently. Stop the music if you need to make a comment. Avoid talking over the music.

- Find music from song bowls on YouTube. Also consider music that blends the sounds of nature and instruments like a harp, piano, or guitar. Music without words is more soothing than music with words. Music with words engages the language pathways of our brains. There are definite benefits to songs with words and singing along to song lyrics. Be sure that there is a mix.

Allow students to wear noise cancelling headphones.

- Encourage parents to remove cell phones from the area where students are doing homework.

- Explain that conflicting sound when learning creates cognitive burnout. This causes neurological fatigue as the school day progresses.

- Make sure there is time in your lesson when you are NOT talking. Silence truly is golden.

Some days your lesson/class can be noisy. Other days your lesson/class should be quiet. Mix it up. In the beginning you may find it helpful to keep track in your lesson plans.

The following activities speak to spending less time with social media. They all focus on imagination and/or being something others want us to be, which is a common problem on social media.

Imagine That...

"Dragons are too seldom."

What do you think this quotation means?

What is "too seldom" in your life? Be specific.

What is "too seldom" in the world? Be specific.

The Land of Everything...

Once upon a time, in the Land of Everything, the birds sang sweetly, the trees touched the bright blue sky, the flowers bloomed all year long and the sun always shone. It was a land where football players never got injured, baseball players hit only home runs, and there was enough food, money, and chocolate for everyone.

Tell a story about the Land of Everything

Describe the Land of Everything. Also, where/when does the story take place?

Use this information to develop the plot of the story. What happens? How? Why? Who does it happen to? What's the conclusion?

Playing the Part...

What images do you create for other people so they will like you? How do you change your personality so that you fit in with different groups of people?

Consider: your family, someone you've never met before, your teacher, a person you haven't see for a long time…

Halloween...

People wear many different masks to cover up parts of their personalities. A mask can "make" people see what is not really there or it can hide a person's inner self from the rest of the world. A mask that protects or covers up someone's "real" personality is called a PERSONA. What masks do you wear? When do you wear them? How does wearing a mask make you feel? How do people react to your masks? Does wearing a mask make it harder or easier to be you?

#6

Generally, students should only work on screens for 30 minutes at a time (less for prepubescent children). In between working with screens, provide a mindful activity (deep breaths, pin wheel breathing, coloring, some yoga).

Strategies for monitoring screen time...

- Tell the students why it is important to monitor screen time in school.

- Use a sand timer. Give a student the responsibility for maintaining the time.

- Set a timer on the SMART Board or on your cell phone.

- Pinwheel Breathing – Hold a pinwheel in front of your face. Inhale through your nose. Count how long it takes to completely fill your lungs with air. Get to know your inhale number. Then exhale through your mouth while moving the pin wheel. Try to double your inhale number with your exhale number.

- Classroom yoga – keep it simple. Trauma informed yoga is not the same as your adult yoga class. Be careful with inversions and poses like downward dog. Some brains want to be inverted and others do not. However, all students benefit from sitting cross legged on the floor or on top of a desk. Wait for quiet.

Regulation

When children have overactive amygdala and a heightened stress response system, they need to learn to regulate these systems. Teachers need to learn about the limbic system and explicitly teach it to their students. When students understand why they lose their patience or become angry, they are better able to do something about it. There are some excellent resources out there to teach about the limbic system and provide suggestions for regulation activities. The *MindUp* curriculum (available from Nathan Levy Books LLC) provides developmentally appropriate lessons for K-2, 3-5, and 6-8 graders.

Regulation in the Classroom

Regulation Space

Create a space in the classroom for children to participate in regulation activities. A chill out space, keep calm corner, or place of peace can be created as needed. This space can be temporary or a permanent place in your classroom. Teach the children to use the space. The regulation space should be a place where children can go to actively work to regain control of their emotions. When children demonstrate the need for regulation, encourage them to consider going there. Keep in mind that this should not turn into the corner of shame where students are sent. Not all students will find the keep calm corner helpful. Some teachers may notice that one of their students takes up residence in the place of peace. If you know this child has been exposed to trauma, make a plan to increase the time that the student is able to work in the general classroom space. Be patient. Work with the student to increase engagement in classroom activities.

Regulation Tools

In addition to a chill out space, all classrooms need to be equipped with regulation tools. Regulation tools can be anything that aids in the regulation of our stress response system. Some tools that have shown to be durable and effective include glitter wands, silicone sponges, fuzzy sticks, and silly putty. Try to include tactile and visual regulation items.

When rolling out the use of regulation tools, keep in mind the following:

- Teachers must have a firm understanding of the reason students benefit from the use of regulation tools.
- Regulation tools are not a reward or consequence.
- Students must be taught about their brain before the roll out of tools.
- Students should be explicitly taught about the tools and how they are to be used.

Many teachers practice utilizing classroom management techniques related to mindfulness. An example of a mindfulness technique is a "Brain Break" which provides students with an opportunity to recognize their mental fatigue, and then refocus or refresh their mindset by implementing an activity that focuses on students mental or physical needs. As we know, this is to provide an opportunity for the amygdala of the child's brain to respond less, which is when the hippocampus begins to activate. These breaks are important for the hippocampus to begin revving up as the child's brain gets ready for self-regulation, memory, and language development.

Typically, "Brain Break" activities are written on cards that are visible and accessible to students in the classroom (i.e. "Brain Break" cards can be placed in a bin and stored in a "Calm Down Corner" in the classroom). "Brain Breaks" can be whole group or individualized activities that help students recenter themselves to regain a sense of calmness. "Brain

Breaks" provide disengaged students with an opportunity to reset into a learning-ready headspace. Provided below are examples of "Brain Breaks:"

Close your eyes and think about how you are feeling. Are you excited? Tired? Happy? Mad? Nervous? Some other feeling? Think of why you are feeling this way.

Close your eyes and think about your body. Feel your feet, then your legs. Concentrate on your stomach as you are breathing in and out. Finally, feel your back, shoulders, face and top of your head. Continue to breath in and out feeling each breath.

Think about something that happened this week. Try and remember everything about that moment. Who was there? How did each person participate? What were your surroundings? What noises did you hear? How did it make you feel?

Close your eyes and take a deep breath in through your nose and out through your mouth. Continue to breathe deeply, taking time to focus on your breathing and how it feels. Now, think of your favorite color or a color that you really like. When you breathe in, focus on breathing in that color. Let this symbolize bringing positive things into your day and into your life. When you exhale, imagine that you are breathing out a color that you do not like. Let that symbolize breathing out the negative things in your day and in your life. Continue to breathe deeply, focusing on breathing the colors that you have chosen in and out. When you are finished, take one last deep breath in through your nose and out through your mouth and slowly open your eyes.

#7

Give students the opportunity to take notes and respond to verbal prompts in writing. On paper. Handwritten work aides in recall better than typed activities and notes.

(Use caution with children who struggle with dyslexia and graphomotor delay.)

Strategies for incorporating writing on paper…

- Computers, laptops, and chrome books are excellent teaching and learning tools. They cannot replace the brain development achieved from reading and writing with paper.

- Make sure your students have a choice to write on paper sometimes.

- For younger students, be sure to vary the style of paper. More lines, less lines, no lines.

- Allow students (in all grades) the opportunity to draw their ideas before they write. This is also a great way to help them increase their details and descriptive language.

Muppet-isms...

"Never eat more than you can lift." - Miss Piggy

What is the heaviest meal you have ever eaten? Describe it and explain what made it so heavy.

"It's not easy being green." - Kermit the Frog

Why not? In what situations would it be okay to be green? What color are you on your best days? What color are you on your worst days? Explain your choices.

Who?

Who is...

Jenny Lind?   Clark Gable?

Alexander Fleming?   Nikita Khrushchev?

James Polk?

Have you heard of these people? If you have, write down what you know. If you have not heard of them, choose three of the names and make up things about them.

1. Describe what this person looks (looked) like. Also, give some interesting facts about this person.
2. Where and when does (did) this person live?
3. What is (was) this person's occupation? Why is this person famous?

*After you complete your work, look up the people you chose and find out who they are (were).

Sunny Days...

Almost everyone watched Sesame Street when they were little.

Remember...

> Cookie Monster
> Grover
> Big Bird
> Ernie
> Bert
> Oscar the Grouch
> The Count
> Kermit

1. Which Muppet from Sesame Street are you most like? Explain.

2. Which Muppet are you least like? Explain.

3. If Jim Henson (the creator of the Muppets and Sesame Street) was going to create a new Muppet based on you, what would this new Muppet be like? Describe in detail, including name and his/her personality traits.

*Hint: This is easier if you make a list of words that describe you and then create the Muppet from your list.

Illustrate this new Muppet.

Early Childhood...

Most people have heard:

> "Sticks and stones can break my bones but names can never hurt me."
> And

> "If you can't say something nice about someone, don't say anything at all."

Based on your experience, tell whether or not these are true.

#8

Children who doodle or color remember more when asked to listen to uninteresting material. This is probably true for interesting material as well.

Strategies for incorporating coloring …

- Students should have access to doodling or coloring. We now know that coloring increasing our ability to understand and connect with auditory information.

- Occasionally a student might struggle to color and listen attentively. One size fits one. In the beginning of each year, give the class paper to doodle or coloring pages. Read a paragraph from a book. Then ask questions and determine which students were able to attend and which students were not. Students who do not attend while coloring may still benefit from coloring when they are stuck on a problem or task, or when they become dysregulated.

- Color during faculty meetings and professional development. If you are tired from a long day of teaching, you will not have to struggle to stay awake if you are coloring. During a multi-hour workshop, you will remember more and feel less tired at the end of the day if you color or doodle throughout the training.

#9

Explicitly teach children to study, as early as first grade. Model and role play are excellent.

Strategies for teaching students to study and learn …

- Do not take it for granted that every student has a parent who helps them set up a homework space that has good lighting and is free from distractions. Review this with parents during Open House. Send home a worksheet explaining how to do this for parents who are unable to attend Open House.

- Teach students to study using each modality. Read the information, write the information, draw a picture of the information, explain the information to someone else.

- Take breaks …
- Use a keyword to refocus yourself …
- Take good notes in class. ...
- Rewrite your notes at home. ...
- Make things interesting. ...
- Study hard subjects first. ...
- Study the important vocabulary. ...
- Make a study group.
- Review often. Develop a study timetable to review your notes each day after class.
- Understanding is the key. Some students try to memorize everything they read without trying to understand.
- Use different materials.
- Make flash cards.
- Take breaks.

An example of Debra Ericksen's (a teacher in central New Jersey) lesson plan for teaching study skills to her grade four students.

Study Skills Lesson Plan

Objective:

Students will be able to identify important information in text and use it to make study cards that reinforce concepts and vocabulary.

Teacher Note: I use this lesson plan for the first time when students are preparing for their first summative assessment in Life Science.

Procedures:

- Explain that over the next few days students will have an opportunity to review science concepts that they have been working with. They will be able to use their science notebooks, investigation recording sheets, text, and the study guide in order to help them review. Explain that it is important to learn how to study because it is not a skill that generally occurs naturally. Ask: How many of you have heard from a teacher or parent, "You need to study better!"? But what does that mean? What does studying look like and feel like?
- Distribute the Life Science Study Guide. Students will work with a partner, independently, or in a guided small group to complete the study guide. (Complete for homework if not done in class.)
- Teacher will model how to create note cards that will support studying by selecting a statement from the Study Guide. Teacher demonstrates how to generate a question from the statement and then write the answer on the other side of the index card.

- Teacher selects another statement or vocabulary word and students help create the card. Then, they create their own card based on the class model.
- Teacher distributes five index cards (more if students want them) and explains that students will now be able to create their own study cards to help them review the content they have been working with in science. They start working in class and finish them for homework. Students bring in the cards the next day.
- Students create another five cards a day or two later. Process can continue depending on how much time there is between the end of the unit and assessment. (I generally plan for a week between to provide for study skills lessons.)

Materials: Study Guide, science notebooks, investigation recording sheets, copies of text (if used in the unit)

Differentiation: small group instruction to support the development of note cards

Assessment: note cards completed according to directions; student's identification of important information

Directions for Making Study Note Cards

Making and using note cards to help you study concepts you have learned is very helpful. With a partner, you will each make your own cards to help you study for the science assessment and to review everything that we have learned about.

Materials Needed: Study Guide, index cards, pencil

1. Write a vocabulary word or a question on the front of the index card.

2. On the back of the index card, write the answer.

For students in middle and high school, many educators teach their students to use Cornell style notes to teach study skills and note taking. The philosophy behind Cornell style notes is to engage the students in recording information, asking questions, reciting valuable information, reflecting upon information and its importance (relevance: strategy 2), and review. Template example below:

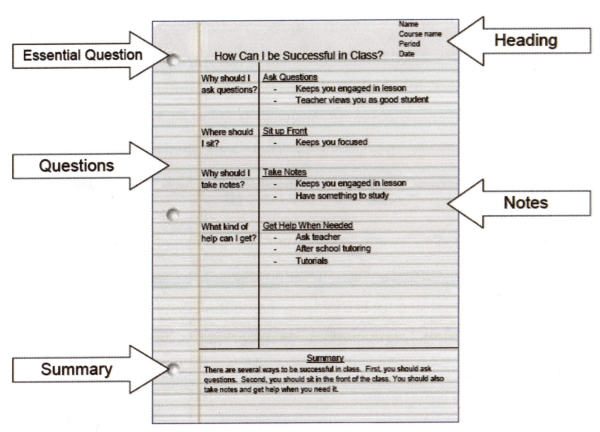

https://felician.libguides.com/c.php?g=557711&p=3835495

Problem-solving...

How would you solve the following problems? Be specific.

1. You and your brother or sister both need to use the home computer for homework.

2. You are riding in a car with an adult who is smoking. The smoke is bothering you.

3. You need to use a book for a school project that someone has already checked out of the library.

Along with teaching students healthy and effective study skills, it is of paramount importance to instill a growth mindset. According to Carol Dweck, people develop a self-perception or "self-theory" about themselves. There are two main mindsets, fixed mindset and growth mindset. An individual with a fixed mindset essentially believes that their traits or talents are inherent and unchangeable. An individual with a growth mindset believe that they can develop talents from dedication and hard work. It is critical for educators to model a growth mindset to students, as it enables them to believe that inner change is possible with commitment and devotion to bettering themselves. Provided below are examples of how to implement growth mindset techniques inside the classroom. The visuals provided below encourage students to never give up and to continue working hard.

#10

Retrieving just learned information increases cognition and memory. This aides in comprehension, increases motivation, serves to anchor information for children with language processing delays and dyslexia, and helps children organize their thoughts around a topic.

Strategies for retrieving just learned information

Ask students to tell a friend what they just learned.

Think pair share and turn and talk.

Ask students to restate or summarize the lesson topic.

A quick exit ticket is useful for retrieving just learned information.

Before this lesson I _____

Now I _____

(For younger children you can ask more specific questions.)

At the end of the school day, ask the student to explain three things he or she learned that day. As they are able to provide three quality answers, increase the number of "learnings" they need to explain for the day.

After a special event (field trip, assembly) have the student recall the activities that occurred.

Give the student a list of description words and have them come up with their opposite.

Help the student use memory aids in order to recall words or actions.

Have the student outline, highlight, underline, or summarize the information.

Create ample opportunities for repetition of information through different experiences

Teach students to rely on resources in his/her environment (notes, textbooks, pictures, etc.)

#11

Check for understanding by having children restate what they understand and/or have learned.

Strategies for checking for understanding…

- Avoid asking "Does everyone understand?" Ask children to restate your point or the directions. Allow classmates to add to what a student says or restate in their words.

- Use visuals or anchor charts that remain available as students work. This supports children with language delays, working memory weakness, auditory processing challenges, etc. (Many children with trauma have these issues as a result of the delay in the growth of the hippocampus.)

#12

Activating the hippocampus aides in memory. Tell jokes or surprise students before practicing math or spelling. (Some children with trauma histories can be triggered by surprises. Use caution.)

As a former teacher, I used to share one joke with my students at the end of each school day. Most of the jokes (examples below) were silly and "not necessarily funny" as some of my former students would suggest. Yet each joke produced laughs, even if out of pity. The most interesting part is that after a few weeks, students started asking if they could share their own jokes. It became a ritual in class that students would submit their jokes in writing by Thursday morning. On Friday, a few submitted jokes (only grammatically correct and school appropriate) were selected to be shared with the class. This created a culture where students could not wait for Friday to share their jokes. As more students wanted to participate, we increased the number of days they would share to every day of the week. This improved classroom culture, writing ability, and engagement as some lessons stemmed from the most popular jokes. I share this example to ease anyone out there that is not 'funny'. It will benefit your students and the connections you make with them. You do not have to be "funny." You simply have to engage and try. - J.Singagliese

What is brown and sticky?

- A stick

Where did the general put his armies?

- In his sleevies

Two fish are in a tank. One looks over to the other and says…"Do you know how to drive this thing?"

#13

Curiosity aides in learning. Many children with trauma struggle with curiosity. It can be explicitly taught in activities across the curriculum. (The Stories with Holes series works well for this. See p. X).

Many of our children are exposed to a mosaic of cultures in their classrooms. This is wonderful as all students need "windows and mirrors." In other words, it is important for children to be introduced to others that are similar and different from them. Being educated in diverse communities helps to enhance a young person's appreciation for various cultures and art. Most importantly, it helps prepare them for living in a global society.

Passport...

List four places around the world you would like to paint or photograph. Explain your choices.

Compass Points...

Choose 2, Write a paragraph for each.
Describe…
…where you first saw prejudice
…where I first new the meaning of emptiness
…where I first saw compassion

Alone...

You are cast away on an island that has an ample supply of food and adequate shelter. As far as you know, there are no other people living there. Which of these 6 items would you want to have on the island with you? Explain.

1. Playing cards
2. Teddy bear
3. Dictionary
4. Pants
5. Football
6. Comb
7. Calculator
8. $100 bill
9. Tomato seed
10. Mirror
11. Pencil and paper
12. Voice recorder

Space Ambassadors...

You have been given the responsibility for selecting five people from the list of volunteers below who are to be sent as the first representatives from the planet Earth to a planet in a distant galaxy. When making your choices, do not worry about problems such as language, life support systems, medical emergencies or enemy attacks...these have all been taken care of by modern technology. List the five people you have chosen and give your reasons for choosing each person.

The Volunteers:

Catholic Priest, white, 29 years old

Model for TV commercials, female, 23 years old

Principal, urban high school, 43 years old

Lawyer, male, black, 35 years old

Editor, national magazine, female

Army major, male, 56 years old

Suburban housewife, mother of 3 children, 32 years old

High School Dropout, male, 18 years old

Professional football player, 24 years old

Child, 12 years old

Doctor, female

Ex-convict, 40 years old

War veteran, 35 years old

Handicapped male confined to wheelchair, 25 years old

Professor of English, University of Massachusetts

Grandmother, 62 years old.

It would probably be easier to decide if there were more data available on these volunteers, but in today's world people are continually forced to make judgements based upon incomplete data. Do your best.

Frozen in Time...

What would happen if time stopped today?

What would the rest of your life be like?

What are some things that would be good about it?

What are some things that you would feel badly about missing out?

Wish You Were Here!

What would you miss if you moved away?

Write about the people, places, and things you would miss the most.

Science Times: Mars Searches for Intelligent Life on Earth...

Is intelligent life found? If so, where? If not, why not, and where has the search led? Write a news story to go along with the headline.

Fun City...

Imagine that in the year 2100 there are specialized cities that are visited exclusively for fun. Everything in the city is for the purpose of entertaining kids. Write a detailed description of "Fun City." Include what the city looks like as well as the kinds of things you can do there.

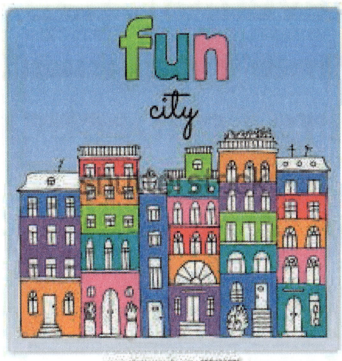

#14

Teachers who discuss what they have in common with their students from other cultures help close the achievement gap. (There are excellent literature connections here.)

Strategies for making connections with students…

- Being connected to your students means knowing five things outside of their academic profile. Teachers should not expect to be connected to all of their students. It takes a village.

- Think about your favorite teacher. Odds are that this was a person who made a connection to your race, religion, culture, socio-economic background, hobby, etc.

- Keep a list of your students. Each week connect to two to three of them. Even if it takes months, make the effort. Your students will learn more if they are connected to you. Your students with trauma will feel safe with you.

- Display a map and let students put a pin in the part of the world they or their ancestors come from.

- If you have students who are refugees or recent immigrants, take the time to find out about their country of origin.

- A great staff activity to make sure all of your students are connected to an adult in the school is called "Connect the Dots."

In November, bring the staff together. Review the meaning of connection. Connection is knowing five things about a student outside of his/her academic profile. Remind teachers that they cannot be connected to all of their students. Each teacher is given five dots. Prior to the meeting, create posters with thumbnail photos of each student in your school. The pictures are arranged in rows with plenty of space between them. The posters are hung on the walls around the room. For a large staff, you can break this down by grade level. The teachers walk around the room placing dots below any student in the school to whom they feel connected. When all the dots have been placed, look around the room. The dots make bar graphs for connection. Find the students with no dots. As a group, discuss who might be willing to make a connection with a particular student. At a follow up faculty meeting take time to check in on the teachers and their new "friends." Occasionally, a teacher will report that their attempts at connecting are not working with a particular student. Find another staff member to give it a try.

Another activity that is excellent for high schools -

Most schools have a data collection system such as PowerSchool, Genesis, or Frontline. All student data is collected in that system. Most schools keep a record of the students who participate in the many clubs and sports offered to high school students. Run the list of students in clubs and sports against the entire student population. What falls out will be a list of students who do not participate in anything. Find those students. Make a connection. Maybe they can be convinced to participate in a club or have lunch with a mentor. Over time, you will find that there are less students coming out as not connected when you run the list through your data system.

The following activities are designed to produce involvement of all participants and to promote feelings of success in both individualized and group settings. The activities provide an opportunity for students to develop imagination and intuition, promote divergent thinking, and afford an opportunity for participants to share experiences and thoughts that enhance connections from students to learning.

I Knew It!

"There are times when I know what's going to happen…"

1. How is it possible to predict the future?
2. How does knowing what is going to happen make you feel before and after it happens?
3. How often can you predict what is going to happen? What does it depend on?
4. What kinds of things can you predict? What kinds of things are impossible for you to predict?
5. Discuss a time when you knew what was going to happen and you were correct. How did you know?

What-Me-Worry…

For each "worry" below, explain what and why it concerns you.

1. A major worry
2. A weird worry
3. A constant worry
4. A one-time-only worry
5. A worry for the future
6. A worry that went away
7. Does worrying help, hurt, or make no difference? Explain

Small Change...

Things in this world are constantly changing. Answer the following questions about "change":

1. How have you changed in the last year? Be specific.
2. What is one change you expect for yourself in the future?
3. What is one change that frightens you?
4. How would you go about trying to change someone's mind?
5. What is something you have changed your mind about?

By the Clock...

Would you rather...be early? Be late? Be on time?

Why?

Does your preference change with the situation?

Don'ts...

What don't you want to be when you grow up?

Discuss how you don't feel today?

What didn't you do this summer?

A Celebration...

1. What holiday do you most like to like to celebrate? Why?
2. In what ways do you celebrate yourself?
3. What is something you think people should celebrate (that you do not ordinarily celebrate)?

Day Off...

If you could have Thursdays off for thinking, what would you think about? Be specific.

#15

Avoid creating cognitive strain.

Strategies for avoiding cognitive strain…

- Do not read the directions aloud while students are reading them silently. Give the directions, then hand out the activity. Wait silently while students read. Then ask for questions and check for understanding. Be sure to have a visual representation of the important points on the board or anchor chart.

- If you play soft music, avoid talking over it. Stop the music, speak to the class, turn the music back on. Music without words is better for our brains during learning activities.

- Allowing students to doodle or color during class will reduce the buildup of cognitive strain as they go through their day.

- Alternate the sound in your classroom. Have silent activities. Have small group activities. All of either one is not good for our brains.

- Provide regulation tools such as glitter wands, silicone sponges, and fuzzy sticks. Use of regulation tools can reduce the sensory overload that impacts many students as their school day progresses.

An example of the directions for the use of a regulation toolbox.

Designed by Julie Young at Riverview Elementary School in Spotsylvania, VA

An example of a choice wheel used in a cool down corner in Spotsylvania, VA. The wheel is on the wall of the cool down corner provided in the classroom. Students can be encouraged to use the corner, or they can choose to go there on their own.

An example of another choice wheel used in Spotsylvania, VA. This one is for upper elementary students.

Hesitation...

"The greatest deterrent to doing anything is trying to do it well."

1. What do you think this quotation means?
2. Do you agree with it? Why or why not?
3. Tell about one thing you did not do because you were afraid you could not do it well enough.
4. Do you think there is any truth to the saying: "Practice makes perfect?"

Keep on Growing...

"People don't grow up because they want to, they grow up because they have to."

1. What does this mean? Explain.
2. When you grow up, what are you "growing up to?"
3. Explain the difference between inside and outside growth.
4. Some people say "Youth is wasted on the young." Why do you think people might feel this way?
5. What does it feel like to grow? Sit very still and try to feel your hair or your fingernails grow.
6. How can you help your mind grow? Describe how you feel before and after you have spent a lot of time studying or reading a book.

Revolving Door...

"The answer is that the answer changes." - Mason Williams

1. What do you think this quotation means?
2. Do you agree with it? Why or why not?
3. Write an answer that you hope will stay the same for you in years to come.
4. Write an answer that you hope will change for you in years to come.

Time Out...

"Time is...too slow for those who wait.

    ...too swift for those who fear

    ...too long for those who grieve

    ...too short for those who rejoice

But for those who love...Time is NOT." - Henry Van Dyke

1. What does this quote mean? Explain.
2. What do you think about "time" in your life? When do you notice it most?
3. Pick two of the above statements about time and think about them in relation to your world. Show how the statement you have chosen is true or has been true in your life.

The Game of Life...

1. What is a game?

2. What makes a game fun? Interesting?

3. What makes a game easy or hard to play? Which do you like playing more--a hard game or an easy game?

4. What is chance? Do you like to play games of chance or skill? Why?

5. "Life is a game-you have to learn the rules in order to play." How is life like a game? How do you learn the rules? What happens if you do not "play" by the rules?

6. What games do you play? Think in terms of "life games."

*Hint - Examine your relationships with people.

#16

You may not want to make students look at you when answering complex questions based on the following findings. *Eye contact drains our more general cognitive resources.*

Strategies for allowing students to avert their gaze while listening or speaking…

- In one study, children answered complex questions correctly only 50 percent of the time when forced to look at someone. ***Their scores improved significantly when they were allowed to avert their gazes.*** This is also true for adults. (http://www.sciencedirect.com/science/article/pii/S0010027716302360).

- Allowing students to color or doodle can enhance their cognitive engagement and their verbal responses during lecture and small group activities.

Tomorrow…

Write three things you would most like to know about your future. Explain why you would like to know them. (The "future" could be tomorrow, one hundred years from now, or anything in between.)

Start, Stop...

Is it easier for you to begin or end things?

26 Hours a Day...

Have you ever felt that there are not enough hours in the day to do all that you want and/or need to do? If you had two more hours every day, what would you do with them? Be specific.

#17

Cautiously use multiple choice quizzes. Having a list of incorrect possible answers next to correct ones can inadvertently help students learn the wrong things.

Garbage...

1. What can garbage tell you?

2. What does your school throw away? Investigate.

3. What does your family throw away? Investigate.

4. Make a "Garbage List" that indicates "valuable" garbage that is thrown out by your school (or your family).

5. Describe an idea that you once "threw out." Explain why you discarded it.

6. Are people ever "thrown away?" Explain.

Stop Sign...

How do you know when to stop? Discuss. Consider: when you stop studying, eating, sleeping, running, liking, asking...

#18

There are two basic ways to teach vocabulary.

Strategies for teaching vocabulary...

- The first is repetition. Using a word often makes it become part of normal vocabulary. (It is why little children can learn the word elephant even though it's a long word.)

- The second way is having children act out the definition. Both the observers and the actors remember the word when next encountered.

The Endless Highway...

Which of these road signs are you most like? Explain your choice.

Stop	Caution
Divided Highway	No U-turn
Speed Limit 55	One Way Street
Pay Toll	Exit
Rest Area	Curve Ahead
Falling Rock Zone	Slippery When Wet
Railroad Crossing	Emergency Stopping Only
Yield	Hitchhikers Prohibited
Do Not Enter	Freeway

Which road sign are you LEAST like? Why?

Create a new road sign for yourself and discuss how it fits you.

#19

Praising struggling learners for mediocre work damages their confidence and their trust and may speed up academic disengagement.

Strategies for authentic and specific praise…

- Feedback that is specific and critical and articulates an instructor's belief in her students' abilities elevates writing performance.

- I noticed…

- Instead of "You look pretty" try, "I am glad you are here".

- "I like your shoes," instead of "You have nice shoes".

- Your use of verb tense in this paragraph is excellent!

Turn, Turn, Turn…

"For everything there is a season and a time for every purpose under heaven."

When is there a time to:

- Weep, and a time to laugh?
- Break down, and a time to build up?
- Keep silent, and a time to speak?
- Seek, and a time to lose?
- Mourn, and a time to dance?
- Keep, and a time to cast away?
- Love, and a time to hate?

Boys-Girls...

1. Boys are not nurses.

2. Boys are better at math than girls.

3. Girls cook better than boys.

4. Girls are less violent than boys.

5. Pink is a girl's color and blue is a boy's color.

6. Boys do not cry as easily as girls do.

7. Girls take care of children better than boys do.

8. Boys are better athletes than girls.

9. Girls are more interested in looking good than boys.

10. Boys manage money better than girls.

These are assumptions made by some people in our society. They might be true or they might be false. You must decide what is TRUE or FALSE for you. For each assumption, do you believe it is true or false for you? Explain your position and give support for answer.

Us...

"Don't walk in front of me - I may not follow. Don't walk behind me - I may not lead. Walk beside me - And just be my friend."

1. What does this quotation mean?

2. What do you need from a friend?

3. What are you able to give to a friend?

4. From your experience, tell why people become friends.

5. A true friendship is an equal partnership. Do you agree? Explain.

#20

Vocabulary expansion activities are a great way to improve writing even when children are not working on a specific writing assignment.

Strategies for vocabulary expansion…

- Instead of using the word "said", challenge children to use more effective synonyms like spoke, proclaimed, reminisced, espoused.

- Teach your students to use their technology to find synonyms.

The following three activities focus on students describing feelings, characteristics of people, places, things, and using their senses to describe. All these tasks expand on vocab.

Relationships…

Tell about the history of a friendship or the history of a rivalry.

- What are the origins of the relationship? How did you meet this person? Where? When?
- Describe the person involved. When you describe things that you "feel" about the person, label by saying "In my opinion."
- Discuss at least three separate events that have contributed to how you feel about this person.
- What is your role in the relationship? What role does the other person have in the relationship? (Consider: dominance, responsibility, age, leadership, knowledge.) What do you get out of the relationship? What does the other person get?
- Would you like to change your relationship with this person in any way? If so, how? If not, why?

Up and Down...

1. Stand on a chair and look down. Describe one thing you see from a "bird's eye view."

2. Sit on the floor, look up, and describe one thing you see from an "ant's eye view."

3. Tell about the differences you experienced when you were "tall" and when you were "short." Include how you felt about each experience. Explain.

Nature Walk...

1. Describe the smell of the earth.
2. Describe the temperature of the water.
3. Describe the color of the sky.

Be specific using your sense of smell, sight, and touch.

ABOUT THE AUTHORS

Melissa Sadin, Ed.D.

Executive Director: Ducks & Lions: Trauma Sensitive Resources
Program Director: Creating Trauma Sensitive Schools for The Attachment & Trauma Network
Special Ed. Director: Unity Charter School

Melissa has served as a special education teacher and a building administrator. She is currently working as a director of special education. Publicly, Dr. Sadin has been vice-president of her local School Board, is on the Board of Directors of the Attachment & Trauma Network and serves as the director of the Creating Trauma Sensitive Schools Program. She is a published author who produces numerous webinars on children with attachment trauma in schools. Currently, Dr. Sadin works as an education consultant and developmental trauma expert providing professional development to school districts, municipal service providers, and parents. As an adoptive mother, Dr. Sadin has provided first hand expertise in her work with adoptive parents at conferences and in other formal and informal settings.

Nathan Levy

Author & Consultant
President, Nathan Levy Books, LLC

Nathan Levy is the author of more than 60 books which have sold almost 500,000 copies to teachers and parents in the United States, Europe, Asia, South America, Australia and Africa. His unique <u>Stories with Holes</u> series continues to be proclaimed the most popular activity used in gifted, special education and regular classrooms by thousands of educators. An extremely popular, dynamic speaker on thinking, writing and differentiation, Nathan is in high demand as a workshop leader in school and business settings. He has worked as a school principal, district supervisor, gifted coordinator, is a company president, parent of four daughters and management trainer. Nathan's ability to transfer knowledge and strategies to audiences through humorous, thought provoking stories assures that participants leave with a plethora of new ways to approach their future endeavors. Nathan Levy Books, LLC is pleased to be the publisher of this book. More books available at www.storieswithholes.com

Dr. James Singagliese

Principal, Adjunct Professor, Author

Dr. Singagliese has over ten years of experience as a principal in both the private and public sector for students in grades pre-kindergarten through high school. Prior to becoming an administrator, he taught at the elementary and middle school levels. He currently is a principal of an elementary school in central New Jersey and an adjunct professor at the College of Saint Elizabeth.

Dynamic Speakers

Creative Workshops

Relevant Topics

Nathan Levy, author of the *Stories with Holes* series, *Teachers' Guide to Trauma* and *Creativity Day By Day* and other nationally known authors and speakers, can help your school or organization achieve positive results with children. We can work with you to provide a complete in-service package or have one of our presenters lead one of several informative and entertaining workshops.

Workshop Topics Include:

- Differentiating in the Regular Classroom
- How to Help Children Read, Write and Think Better
- Powerful Strategies to Enhance the Learning of Gifted Students
- Powerful Strategies to Help Hard to Reach Students Become More Successful Learners
- Teachers' Guide to Trauma
- Arts and Resiliency
- Gifted and Trauma
- Brain Whys – How the Brain Works
- Adoption Competent Education
- IEP/504 Facilitation
                    and many more…

Please write or call to receive our current catalog.
Nathan Levy Books, LLC
(732) 605-1643
NLevy103@comcast.net
www.storieswithholes.com

Unique Materials Published by
Nathan Levy Books, LLC

A.C.T. 1: Affective Cognitive Thinking

Artistry

Beyond Schoolwork

Brain Whys

Breakfast for the Brain

Creativity Day-By-Day

Gifted Children and How Trauma Impacts Them

Nathan Levy's Intriguing Questions – Volumes 1-6

Nathan Levy's Stories with Holes – Volumes 1-22

Nathan Levy's Test Booklet for Every American

Perfectionism vs. the Pursuit of Excellence

Principles of Fearless Leadership

School Leaders' Guide to Trauma Sensitive Schools

Teachers' Guide to Resiliency Through the Arts

Teachers' Guide to Trauma

The Principals Recommend: 101 Great Activities for Student
  Learning and Brain Development

There Are Those

Thinking & Writing Activities for the Brain- Bks 1 & 2

THINKology

Trauma Informed Teaching Strategies That Are Good For All

What To Do When Your Kid is Smarter Than You

Whose Clues? (Am. Hist., Mus., Lit., Sci., Sports, Authors)

Write from the Beginning

Ducks & Lions: Trauma Sensitive Resources
www.traumasensitive.com

Creating Trauma Sensitive schools for ALL children and the people who serve them.

- Creating Trauma Sensitive Schools - Professional Development
- Train-the-Trainer and Coaching models available
- IEP / 504 Facilitation for parents and schools
- Trauma-Informed Functional Behavior Assessment Services
- Gifted Activities that Work

Melissa Sadin – Executive Director
Melissa.sadin@gmail.com
 @melissasadin